FOREWORD

The name of Aline Bernstein will forever enjoy a stellar position in the annals of the American theatre. Mrs. Bernstein's knowledge of costume design, both historical and theatrical, was second to none and her contributions will long be studied in all languages and wherever theatre has become an integral part of the national life.

It is fitting that this book be published under the auspices of The American National Theatre and Academy, for Aline Bernstein was dedicated to the concept upon which the ANTA Congressional Charter is based. As a member of its Board of Directors she gave unselfishly of her time, talent and effort for the benefit of our organization. This book serves as a fitting memorial to one of the great figures of theatre in the twentieth century.

George Freedley
Secretary, THE AMERICAN NATIONAL THEATRE AND ACADEMY

ALINE BERNSTEIN
An Appreciation

Aline Bernstein began her career at the Neighborhood Playhouse for which she did some of her most poetic and imaginative settings, among them *The Dybbuk* and *The Little Clay Cart*. It was the period shortly before and during the early 1920's that ushered in a renaissance of the American theatre when other so-called "little theatre" groups—the Washington Square Players, the Theatre Guild, the Provincetown and Greenwich Village Theatres—also found new audiences and won recognition for playwrights and designers such as Eugene O'Neill, Elmer Rice and Robert Edmond Jones.

An actor's daughter, born, so to speak, within sight of the footlights, Aline Bernstein inherited a passionate love of the theatre and became one of our leading designers, a position she maintained throughout her long career with her productions, among them *Romeo and Juliet*, *The Cherry Orchard*, *Victoria Regina*, *Ned McCobb's Daughter*, *The Animal Kingdom*, *The Male Animal* and *Grand Hotel*. Whether her staging was stylized or realistic she displayed a sensitive and subtle imagination, the skill of a master craftsman and a passion for perfection, creating an ensemble of setting, costuming and lighting that illuminated the meaning of each play and sustained its emotional and dramatic impact.

As if this were not enough to fill a lifetime, as the author of three volumes, *Three Blue Suits*, *The Journey Down* and *An Actor's Daughter*, she became a distinguished literary figure. She was also an able and indefatigable administrator, originally as a co-founder and a director with Irene Lewisohn and myself of the Museum of Costume Art in 1937 (since 1946 affiliated with the Metropolitan Museum of Art as the Costume Institute) and as its president for ten years until shortly before her death in 1955. Another field of interest was the Poetry Center at the Y.M.H.A. which she sponsored and where she presided at readings by younger and lesser-known poets. Here also young playwrights could try out their experiments in verse form. As a visiting lecturer on costume design at Vassar College and as consultant for its Experimental Theatre productions (among them Cummings' *him* and the American premiere of Sartre's *Les Mouches*), she proved herself an effective and inspiring critic and teacher. The range of her interests was extraordinarily wide and she gave herself to each one with an unselfish and contagious enthusiasm that won her a host of lifelong friends among her pupils and her colleagues.

The plates, in color and in line, of period costumes and their accessories collected in this volume were made under a Rockefeller grant in 1930. In their precision of detail, which recalls the skill of a medieval or Renaissance miniaturist, they display a knowledge of the structure of a costume which, together with the texture and pattern of the materials used, make the characteristic fashion of any historic period. No colored photograph could have rendered these costumes as completely and as accurately to the last and most minute detail of edging, embroidery or ornamentation. I feel sure that a textile manufacturer could, from the colored drawings alone, reproduce any of the materials from which they were made. For Aline Bernstein was not only a costume designer but an expert dressmaker who not only saw the external effect of a dress but understood it literally from the inside out and was able, if necessary, to cut it out of whole cloth and sew it together herself.

This volume should prove invaluable to all students of the history of costume, to costume designers in the theatre and to fashion designers as well. For contemporary fashions are always revivals, a re-interpretation of some elements—cut, draping, embellishment or ornament—of historic styles.

Theatre art is an evanescent art and within a generation or two any production becomes mere memory or a legend. Even if photographs exist, they can at best give only an inadequate idea of a performance as seen and experienced. It is fortunate that Aline Bernstein has left this record of one phase of her art—a lasting legacy.

LEE SIMONSON

Masterpieces of Women's Costume
of the 18th and 19th Centuries

Written and Illustrated by
Aline Bernstein

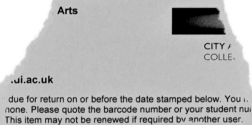
DOVER PUBLICATIONS, INC.
Mineola, New York

Bibliographical Note

This Dover edition, first published in 2001, is an unabridged republication of the book originally published in a limited edition of 2000 copies in 1959 by Crown Publishers, Inc., New York. The only significant alteration consists in retaining the thirty-two color plates in black and white in their original positions in the book, as well as repeating them all in an eight-page full-color insert after page 52.

Library of Congress Cataloging-in-Publication Data

Bernstein, Aline, 1881–1955.
    Masterpieces of women's costume of the 18th and 19th centuries / written and illustrated by Aline Bernstein.
       p. cm.
   Originally published: New York : Crown, 1959.
    ISBN 0-486-41706-9 (pbk.)
     1. Costume—History—18th century. 2. Costume—History—19th century. I. Title.

GT595 .B45 2001
391'.2'09033—dc21

2001017408

Manufactured in the United States of America
Dover Publications, Inc., 31 East 2nd Street, Mineola, N.Y. 11501

INTRODUCTION

Of all the animal kingdom, man alone was not provided by nature with a covering sufficient to protect him from the elements. It is true that in equatorial regions clothing is necessary only for modesty and embellishment, but that is a small section of this earth. Since man's first disobedience, since Eve ate the apple, the covering of the human form has been a problem. Fig leaves were very well at first in the Garden of Eden, but soon something more durable and more voluminous became a necessity. So the ingenuity of the human mind came into play and clothing was invented. At first the skins of wild animals were used, and in warmer countries vegetable matter was transformed into stuffs for covering: covering for the head against the sun, for the feet against the roughness of the ground, and for the body against the eyes of other humans. Presumably modesty came in with the expulsion from Paradise, but we can only surmise. At any rate, what once was only a necessity against heat and cold and exposure has become the concern of all civilized populations in our time, and is a huge trade. Thousands of men and women have put their minds to it. Men have stolen and women have deceived in order to dress according to their fancy.

For centuries clothing probably followed the lines of the form: an opening for the head to come up, coverings for the arms and legs, and a girdle round the middle to keep the garment in place. From such a simple beginning we have made a wide departure, whether in the right or wrong direction it is impossible for me to say. The fact remains that clothing, although still a necessity, has become a social adjunct to life, and an indication to a certain extent of the wealth and status of the wearer.

It would be interesting to know when and how the first best dress came into use, when the man or woman felt that he or she should be singled out from the crowd to be looked at as something extra, something demanding special attention, some special day or hour to be marked. If we knew, we would know more about man and his ego. In the beginning, the something extra might have been a flower behind the ear, or a chaplet of leaves. Then the seams of the garment may have been strengthened and ornamented, then the fabric itself, then came the differentiation of cut. We only know what is recorded, and that is little enough until it occurred to man to scratch on a stone what he saw.

The subject is enormous, not only in the mass of material available for study, but in its implications. Vistas of commercial and of aesthetic values stretch out on all sides, further than the eye of the mind can reach; and for me, the vista of the wonder of man's inventiveness. Each age and each country has had its convention of cut, style, and ornament, and within that convention are a million evidences of the creative mind. With new ideas and designs came new techniques and finer crafts-manship, until there is practically nothing in clothing that cannot be expressed.

The simplest and most unsophisticated peoples have given us our finest costume documents, webs and embroideries of fairylike fineness and designs and colors of magnificent strength. Slaves wove the linen and metal wonders of Egypt, and unlettered women netted the laces for queens. A woman of India spun a thread of such fineness that for fear a breath of air might break it, she sat in a close dark room with but one ray of light entering through a chink in the wall. Peasants spent their long dark winter hours spinning and weaving and embroidering; their coarse hands and their rich minds have left us their record. Wild men, with black skins, have looked at nature and translated her forms into objects and patterns that are today the inspiration of our designers. They are all as anonymous as the stone workers and wood workers who made the mighty cathedrals of ancient times, the weavers and pattern makers of France, Italy, England, Spain and Russia, and the workers who made the untold riches that have come to us from the East. It adds up to more than dress, for here are the aesthetics, and the great bulk of the commerce of nations before science made demands on other materials of earlier times. Food for thought, for ideas, and alas, for wars.

Present in all the documents is evidence of Fashion. You think of fashion as something dating at its earliest from the eighteenth century, when fashion was a rule, not only of dress, but of conduct. But it has always been the fashion of humans to dress, in the main, alike. Fashion may seem to be absurd, but it is a deep-rooted need of man. It is the herd instinct, but when, how, and why fashion changes, that is the mystery. The tribes of darkest Africa have their fashions, whether it is a hairdo or the insertion of a disk into the lower lip, or spirals of brass to lengthen the neck, or carving his own flesh into a design. It was the fashion of the brave men of Scotland to wear a plaid skirt and no breeks, for the men of India to wind their lower limbs intricately in a scarf, instead of trousers, for the Ptolemies to wear too much hair, and for the little ladies of the period of the Napoleonic wars to wear nothing against the cruel winters of the North but the finest muslins, clinging to their wetted thighs. Strangest of all is the fashion that likes to make the human form protrude where it does not do so by nature. The farthingale, the pannier, the hoop and the bustle, the padded shoulder and the leg of mutton sleeve, their origin is in Limbo. People say it is all to make the waist look small, but why make the waist look small? We will never know, nor will we know why it was once the fashion for women to have drooping shoulders and rounded hips and fifty years later it was the fashion to have square, wide shoulders and hips as narrow as a boy of twelve. The female form itself follows the line, too, believe it or not. There is concrete evidence in the size and cut of existing dresses.

It is the object of this book to show, by a selection of typical examples, from the beginning of the eighteenth century to the decade of the 1880's, how these clothes were cut, their fabric, and the framework upon which they were built. It would take a lifetime to go fully into the subject, to draw and analyze all of the material that is available to the interested person. Clothes, like people, look the way they look because they are the way they are, and they have the appearance of their character. I make no attempt to give a history of costume, nor to go into the theory of the effect of political situations upon cut and style and ornament. That has been done; volumes have been written. This practical analysis is merely a statement of fact, expressed as graphically as possible.

Every color plate has been made from a real costume, faithfully drawn and painted. In the black and white plates are the underclothes, the panniers, the hoop skirts, the bustles, the shoes and the hair arrangements that rightly belong to the costumes. Except for an occasional set or piece they are not the things that were actually worn with the dresses. But they are all correctly of the period, and almost all were drawn from the objects. Where the real thing was lacking, the drawings were made from contemporary prints, or fashion books. It was interesting to find so many lovely things preserved. I found them in the large city museums, in private collections, in trunks and attics in old houses, and many of the most interesting in the little museums or historical societies in towns in our Eastern states. The hunt was elusive, and fascinating, and the difficulty was not always in collecting material, but in making a selection from the many lovely things that came to light.

It is difficult—almost impossible—to reproduce a period, complete it in its picture, and in its feeling. Small customs, daily doings, and ways of life have gone unrecorded, even turns of speech; but in reproducing clothes, we have a storehouse of evidence. It needs only to be studied and assembled; no magic is needed to find it but the magic of genuine interest for those people who are looking for this knowledge, and need it. I trust the work set forth in this book will be a help, not only in its content, but in showing a way to further explorations.

ALINE BERNSTEIN

DESCRIPTIONS OF THE PLATES

(For this edition, the thirty-two color plates appear in black and white in their original positions, and in color in an eight-page insert after page 52.)

1-2
ENGLISH, about 1700–1710

1—Color Plate
Brown silk dress. The dress is exquisitely embroidered with white threads, the pattern is supposedly composed of flowers that grew in the gardens of Hampton Court. It is believed that this dress belonged to Queen Anne.

2—Accessories
Hair arrangement, softly rolled back, with puffs at side and long curls hanging to the shoulder, natural color. **Pannier** of metal, hinged to make it flexible, covered with linen and held together with linen tapes. **Petticoat** of warm shade of ecru silk, beautifully quilted, linen top held with a drawstring of linen tape. **Corset** of taupe silk, brocaded with magenta and green, front lacing. **Shoes** of green brocade, many colors, and gold thread.

3-4-5-6
ITALIAN, first half of the 18th Century

3—Color Plate
A dress of soft sage green. The silk is brocaded in grays, cream, darker green and silver, and is trimmed with a gray braid, applied in curved forms. It is from Venice, and is accompanied by typical Venetian accessories.

4—Accessories
Corset of peacock blue satin sewn with rose-colored threads, with rose-colored ribbon trimming, front lacing. **Hat** of black silk plush, tricorne shape, laced with silver. **Mantilla,** black lace, with a netted piece that fits over the head and is worn under the hat. **Gloves** of blue kid, with brown ornament. **Shoes** of black leather, very pointed turned-up toes.

5—Accessories
Hair arrangement, powdered, softly drawn back from the forehead, waved, with curls at the side and nape of the neck. **Mask** of black papier-maché. **Pannier** of hand-woven natural color linen, stiffened with metal, hinged, and tied with linen tapes.

6—Pattern Plate

7-8
FRENCH, last half of the 18th Century

7—Color Plate
Dress of heavily ribbed green silk. The silk is brocaded with a floral pattern in bouquets and running vines, mostly roses, in shades of pink, green, and gold color. The trimming is composed of bands of the silk, laid in box pleats and edged with a dainty open-work galloon of rose and gold threads. The pattern of the silk is called Dauphine, in compliment to Marie Antoinette upon her arrival in France.

8—Accessories
Shift of fine linen, buttoned at front, the ruffles edged with hand-sewn hem. **Pannier** of coarsely woven linen, stiffened with metal. **Shoes** of green silk, brocaded with rose and gold. **Corset** of yellow hand-woven linen; back lacing.

9-10
ENGLISH, middle of the 18th Century

9—Color Plate
Dress of a rich shade of yellow silk. It is embroidered with flowers in a bold design in brilliant colors, the embroidery evidently done on the silk before the dress was made up. The sleeve ruffles are edged with purple ribbon.

10—Accessories
Hair arrangement, drawn up and back from the brow, with two rolls of hair outlining the head; curls at side and nape of neck, tied with a bow. Lightly powdered. **Corset** of red silk, stiffened with reed. Back lacing, and a short front lacing as well. **Petticoat** of green taffeta silk, richly and exquisitely quilted. **The shoes** are of heavy corded green silk with leather heels, accompanied by a clog. The clog is a leather overshoe, used against rain as we use rubbers.

11-12-13
FRENCH, after the middle of the 18th Century

11—Color Plate
Dress of yellow satin. It is a two-piece style, known as the Caraco. The trimming is made of self-material, shirred and tacked through the center to give a rich effect, and edged with a lacy galloon of silk cord and chenille. This was a style of dress much used in the country.

12—Accessories
Petticoat of hand-woven linen, diagonally quilted and with a leafy border, gathered into a deep waistband. **Corset** of brown twill sewn with white thread; a gusset inset to hold the breasts; front lacing. **Pannier** of tan linen, stiffened with metal. **Hair arrangement,** drawn from forehead and knotted at the back, with curls at side. Simple muslin cap.

13—Pattern Plate
Shoes of silk, ribbon-bound.

14-15
ENGLISH, third quarter of the 18th Century

14—Color Plate
Dress of bright coral silk. The silk is a damask, the pattern composed of typical English flowers and shrubs, among them the English holly. The trimming is of self silk, the bands shirred and pinked at the edges. The petticoat showing at the front is of flesh-pink silk, quilted.

15—Accessories
Hair arrangement. Formal; powdered and combed over a foundation, with stiff side curls; a garniture of gauze and pearls at the top. **Pannier** of heavy natural linen, stiffened with metal, and underpetticoat of the same, quilted. **Corset** of plum-colored linen, lined with sage green; back lacing. **Shoes** of ecru ribbed silk, with paste buckles set in gold.

16-17
ENGLISH, last half of the 18th Century

16—Color Plate
Dress of heavy blue satin. The type is known as à la française. The pleated trimming and flounces are of the same satin, embellished with a design of punched work, pinked at the edges. This was a type of decoration much used, and gives a rich and interesting effect.

17—Accessories
Cloak of sapphire-blue velvet edged with fur. **Pannier** of hand-woven linen, stiffened with metal strips. **Shoes** of blue satin to match the gown. **Corset** of yellow silk, brocaded with leaves and

flowers. **Shift** of muslin with pad at the hips. **Hair arrangement,** formal and powdered. It is combed up and over on foundation and puffed at the sides and back, trimmed with pearls, flowers, etc., and topped with a little gauze cap.

18-19
ENGLISH, last quarter of the 18th Century

18—Color Plate
Dress of fine-textured blue silk. The dress is heavily quilted in a rich all-over design. No doubt this dress was worn for informal occasions, possibly for street wear because of its weight. The petticoat is also heavily quilted; it is made of ivory satin that has aged to a beautiful deep shade.

19—Accessories
Shift of fine linen, the flounces and ruffles hemmed by hand. Over it is the corset of deep pink silk bound with red ribbon; front lacing. It shows how constricted the body and breasts were. **Hair arrangement,** waved loosely back from the forehead and curled under; dressed with a ribbon bow. The hair is worn loose at the back and curled under at the shoulder line. **Hat** of natural straw, trimmed with a puff of muslin and pink-and-white striped ribbon. **Shoes** of blue silk.

20-21
FRENCH, very end of the 18th Century

20—Color Plate
Dress of white cotton. The bouquets of flowers are painted on the fabric by hand. Possibly the material was made and painted in India; the flowers are exotic, and do not look like the flowers of France. The dress is most informal and is undoubtedly a country-made piece, inelegant though interesting in cut, and rather clumsily made.

21—Accessories
Linen pocket embroidered in colored silk threads. **Corset waist** of heavy linen, laced up the back and worn over a linen shift. **Hair arrangement,** rolled from the face and curled at the sides and back, with an embroidered muslin cap tied under the chin. **Calash** of thin green silk. **Shoes** of white kid stamped in black, with black leather heels and black ribbon trimming.

22-23
FRENCH, beginning of the 19th Century

22—Color Plate
Dress of white India muslin. The dress is embroidered with a powdering of flower sprays in colored woolen threads. The colors are rich and brilliant, the flowers are conventionalized natural forms. The dress has a long train, which probably marks it as a dress used for the evening.

23—Accessories
Corselet or brassière of heavy linen, closing at side front with two gold buckles, holding the breasts high and firm according to the fashion. **Underdress** of white muslin, the bottom of the skirt trimmed with three rows of saw-tooth braiding. **Pantalettes.** Long, of very sheer muslin, gathered into a band at the ankle and edged with a knife-pleated, hand-hemmed frill. **Shoes** of ivory kid, embroidered with gold and spangles, trimmed and tied with taffeta ribbons.

24-25-26
FRENCH, the Empire Period

24—Color Plate
Dress of sheer white India muslin. The dress has a short train and is embroidered with gold threads of various weights in a running vine-like pattern with occasional single flowers. The workmanship is exquisite. The fabric is so fine—almost a gauze—it seems impossible that it can hold the metal thread.

25—Accessories
Underdress of white muslin with insets and hand netting, simply embroidered, front and back view. **Shoes** of sage-green kid, trimmed and laced with ivory ribbon. **False breasts** of papier-mâché, covered with linen pasted on; held together in the front and tied in the back with linen tapes. These false breasts seemed to be widely used, much as the brassières of today are used to raise the breasts.

26—Pattern Plate

27-28
AUSTRIAN, early 19th century

27—Color Plate
Two dresses. At the right, a dress of web-like linen, embroidered at the hem with silk threads in a simple floral design. At the left, a dress of fine muslin, heavily embroidered at the hem with cotton and metal threads; insets of fine net.

28—Accessories
Reticule. Urn-shaped, made of papier-mâché covered with green silk pasted on, and trimmed with spangles and a chain of steel. **Gloves** of white cotton dimity, fingerless except for the thumb; hand-sewn and stitched on the backs. **Hair arrangement** of the period, known as wind-blown. The hair is cut short and uneven. **Cap** of white muslin, embroidered with white cotton thread. **Shoes** of ivory kid, stamped and further embellished with spangles.

29
Early 19th century

29—Color Plate
Three silk spencers. These little jackets were made of silk, sometimes heavily padded for warmth, and worn over the delicate dresses. There was no end to the variety of color, fabric, design, and ingenuity of trimming in these jackets. The three on this page are from a collection that came from Vienna, but they might well be French.

The upper one is a soft silk, green striped with ecru and wine. It is trimmed with puffings of ribbon and braid, and flowers of ribbon. The center one is dove-gray silk with a tiny Jacquard design, trimmed with puffings of gray satin and folds of plum-colored silk.

The bottom one is of a soft lustrous silk, apricot-colored, with a folded trimming of orchid-colored satin.

30-31-32
ENGLISH, decade of the 1820's

30—Color Plate
Dress of white silk striped with blue, the heavier stripes having a chiné effect. The trimming of cords and leaf shapes is made of a blending blue satin.

31—Accessories
Petticoat of heavy white linen, embroidered with cotton thread in a solid and eyelet embroidery design. **Shift** of fine white linen, the ruffles hemmed by hand. **Corset** of thick white twill, hand-sewn, with back lacing; cup-shaped insets to hold the breasts. **Drawers.** Long, made of white cotton and embroidered. **Shoes** of deep blue kid; square toes.

32—Pattern Plate

33-34-35
ENGLISH, decade of the 1820's

33—Color Plate
Velvet dress of a soft shade of violet. The dress is trimmed with

cords and points of a blending satin, a type of ornamentation much used. The velvet and satin are no doubt of French manufacture. The rather large long sleeve is interesting as a step toward the leg o' mutton sleeves of the coming thirties.

34—Accessories

Corset waist of heavy twill, fine hand-hemmed linen, frills at the top and on shoulder straps. The corset itself is sewn by hand. **Petticoat** of rather heavy linen, embroidered with cotton thread in a solid and English eyelet pattern. **Drawers.** Long, made of linen, embroidered at the ankles. **Shoes** of plum-colored velvet, embroidered with gold and spangles.

35—Pattern Plate

36-37-38
ENGLISH, decade of the 1830's

36—Color Plate

Dress of red moire. This dress is trimmed with pleatings and folds of itself, and bands of saw-tooth trimming. It has the enormous, exaggerated sleeve of the period, which tends to make the waist look very small. The shoulder is so drooped that it seems the arm could have little or no play of movement save for the fact that the sleeve is so roomy.

37—Accessories

Shift of linen cut to fit the body and embroidered at neck and sleeve edge, back and front view. **Petticoat** of white cotton, heavily embroidered with white thread, the pattern very rich and exotic. **Corset waist** of robin's-egg blue twill, sewn by hand with pale pink cotton thread. **Shoes** of bronze kid, trimmed and tied with bronze-colored ribbons. **Hair arrangement,** elaborate, with side-curls, bow-shaped knot.

38—Pattern Plate

39-40
ENGLISH, decade of the 1830's

39—Color Plate

Gray taffeta silk dress. It is ornamented with folds and cordings of itself, the diagonal folds extending from the shoulder to the center of the breasts, typical of this period. The dress is possibly Quaker.

40—Accessories

Corset waist of yellow twill, sewn with thread of a deeper shade in an ornamental pattern. Back lacing. **Hair arrangement,** parted simply and drawn into side puffs; the comb is of tortoise shell. **Shift** of fine white linen, loosely cut and sewn by hand. **Drawers** of heavier linen, long at the legs and embroidered at edges. **Petticoat,** cotton, heavily embroidered. **Shoes** of black silk brocaded with small clusters of silver-gray flowers, laced around the ankle with black ribbons.

41-42-43
AMERICAN, decade of the 1830's

41—Color Plate

Dress of olive-colored silk. This dress is made very wide at the shoulder by the addition of two collars, one above the other, stiffened at their edges by folds and cords, and topped with a fine embroidered muslin collar. The enormous sleeve is tapered and pleated into a cuff with cutout points. These sleeves were often extended by a pillowlike padding, tied to the armhole with tape. The olive tones and all shades of grays and tans were widely used in the thirties.

42—Accessories

Corset waist of heavy white cotton twill, stitched and corded in a fanciful design. Many of these corset waists have a homemade look, and are often dated and initialed by the maker. **Hair arrangement,**

simple and smooth, parted at the center, the hair braided and looped at the sides. **Shift** of softest white muslin, hand-sewn. **Petticoat** of fawn-colored woolen material, resembling mohair or alpaca, heavily padded and quilted to the knee and gathered into a deep boned belt. **Shoes** of a thin woolen cloth, laced at the back and with a pleated frill trimming at the top.

43—Pattern Plate

44-45-46
AMERICAN, about 1845

44—Color Plate

Dress of peach silk. The dress has a very long bodice, rounded at its point. The drooping shoulders are finished by a pleated, fringed bertha. The dress is trimmed with a meandering design of self-color braid on waist and skirt, and further ornamented with sprays of flowers embroidered with ivory silk threads. The skirt is wide and very full.

45—Accessories

Corset of white cotton twill, heavily corded. The top has a band of embroidery and there is a center-front steel-hooked closing, back lacing. **Shift,** white cotton, with fluted ruffles and a delicate vine embroidery. **Shoes** of pink corded silk matching the dress; laced at the side. **Petticoat** of fine mull, with many horizontal tacks run by hand, and finished at the edge with a narrow frill.

46—Pattern Plate

47-48-49
AUSTRIAN, decade of the 1840's

47—Color Plate

Dress of soft green silk. The silk has a woven plaid of wine color. The bodice is long, tight, and slender, and the shoulder is sloping. The dress is trimmed with a narrow, matching green silk passementerie, and sherrings of the silk. The skirt is wide and sewn to the waist band with very fine gauging.

48—Accessories

Corset of white fine twill, embroidered at the top and boned with steel. **Shift** of fine white cotton, embroidered at neck and sleeves. **Drawers,** heavy cotton, embroidered at hems and gathered into a pointed waistband. **Petticoat** of cotton, with three wide tucks going round and a band of very handsome English eyelet embroidery at the bottom. **Shoes** of cloth, laced in front.

49—Pattern Plate

50-51-52
AMERICAN, decade of the 1850's

50—Color Plate

Dress of fancy silk. The silk is white, horizontally striped with groups of bands of powder blue, alternating with bands of flowers in the chiné effect. The type of silk was called pompadour. It has a decidedly French and flowery effect. It is a two-piece style; the bodice with its wide peplum is worn over a very full, straight skirt. The horizontal stripes give the effect of even greater width. The sleeve is puffed at the top, and flowing at the wrist; the bodice is trimmed with a fringed blue passementerie, and is worn with collar and undersleeves of embroidered mull.

51—Accessories

Corset cover of white muslin, trimmed with embroidered bands and puffs. **Corset** of white twill, very closely boned. **Shoes** of pale blue, blending silk, with leather tips and side lacings. **Petticoat** of white muslin, elaborately embroidered with a palm design in English eyelet embroidery extending in a panel up the front. On the waistband of this petticoat is embroidered: *My mother dear, 1855.*

52–Pattern Plate

53-54
ENGLISH, decade of the 1850's

53—Color Plate
Dress of rose-pink and blue shot taffeta silk. The dress is a two-piece style, the bodice is long and pointed in front, with sloping shoulders enhanced by bretelles. The sleeve is open and flowing at the bottom. The peplum is attached to the bodice, and the dress is trimmed with ribbons of blue and rose of a deeper shade. There is a fine white mull embroidered collar at the neck, and undersleeves to match.

54—Accessories
Shift of white cotton, finely embroidered at the yoke and edge of sleeves. **Hair arrangement,** parted at the front, the strands looped around and behind the ears, caught into a knot at the neck. **Corset** of white twill, corded and boned. **Petticoat** of heavy linen, embroidered in a set design in solid and English eyelet embroidery. **Shoes** of very dark eggplant-colored silk, interestingly cut and tied in two places by ribbon passed through eyelets in the silk.

55-56-57-58
FRENCH, about 1858

55—Color Plate
Dress of yellow silk. The silk is embossed with brown velvet in an elaborate design. The silks for this type of dress were woven in what was known as robe-length; that is, enough silk for an entire dress with its accompanying woven bands and borders for trimming was woven and sold entire, not by the yard. It was an extravagant method, and the dresses were of the richest variety and make. The waist has a simple cut and buttons down the front. The shoulders slope, the sleeves are wide and flowing, and the bodice has a pointed front and back and is worn over the skirt. The skirt is elaborate, and is held out by a hoop. English Honiton-lace collar and undersleeves.

56—Accessories
Corset of pink Jacquard silk trimmed with pink plush. Front hook closing, under a plus fly; back lacing. **Drawers** of fine cotton, embroidered. **Shoes** of brown grosgrain silk, with elastic sides; lace-ribbon and buckle trimming. **Hoop** of woven metal wire, covered with a linen web and held together with a beautiful hand-knotting of linen cords.

57—Accessories
Chemise of fine cotton, embroidered by hand. **Hairdress,** parted in the middle and drawn back, the sides braided and held into the back knot. **Petticoat** of a fine muslin, with a double ruffle, embroidered.

58—Pattern Plate

59-60-61
AMERICAN, end of the decade of the 1850's

59—Color Plate
Dress of green silk. The silk is horizontally brocaded with bands of black and white. The shoulders are sloping, the sleeves are wide and flowing at the wrist, and the usual embroidered mull collar and undersleeves are worn. The skirt is extended by a hoop.

60—Accessories
Shift of white muslin, the yoke and upper sleeves of lace and puffings. **Corset** of figured twill, with a steel-hooked front closing. Back lacing. **Drawers** of heavy cotton with embroidered edges. **Petticoat,** cream flannel, embroidered at the edges with a design in white silk threads. **Hoop** of whalebone, held together with wide linen tapes.

61—Pattern Plate with Accessories
Pattern and back view, hair dressed with ribbon ornament. **Shoes** of black cloth, with kid tips and trimmings, stitching of yellow thread, and elastic sides.

62-63
AMERICAN, decade of the 1860's

62—Color Plate
Dress of silk taffeta. The silk is cream-colored with a fine speckled chiné pattern in light tan and is brocaded in red-violet polka dots. The dress is one-piece style, with a high, round fitted bodice, low square neckline and short double puffed sleeves. The skirt is full with a slight train at back, and is worn over a hoop. The dress is trimmed with red-violet satin ribbon which edges the neck, forms the belt, and trims the front of the skirt in a double row of rosettes and a line of satin-covered buttons. Dress opens down front to below the waistline and closes with velvet buttons on the bodice.

63—Accessories
Chemise of white cotton or linen with short sleeves and a deep yoke. **Corset,** stitched, with steel-hooked front closing and back lacing. **Petticoat** of white cotton with a deep border of horizontal and diagonal tucking. **Hoop,** covered and tied across the front. **Shoes,** elaborately trimmed, with rounded toes and low heels. **Hair arrangement,** parted in the middle, the sides braided and looped across the back.

64-65-66
AMERICAN, decade of the 1860's

64—Color Plate
Dress of silk and wool material. The material is woven in a plaid of cream, brown, and tan, and overlaid with a plaid of a fine line of bright cherry-pink. The bodice is tight-waisted with sloping shoulders and very wide flowing sleeves, and trimmed with a ribbon repeating approximately the colors of the dress fabric. The ribbon trimming is used in bretelle shapes at the shoulders, and in bows on the sleeves. The skirt is wide, worn over a hoop, and pleated in to the waist. A collar and undersleeves of lace.

65—Accessories
Corset, boned and machine-stitched; steel-hooked front closing, and back lacing. **Drawers** of cotton, with lace and embroidery trimming, and ribbons tied at knee. **Shoes,** tan cloth, side lacing. **Hoop** or reed, covered and held together with cotton tape.

66—Accessories
Hair arrangement, parted simply in front and held in a snood of silk cord which is beaded at the intersections and trimmed with loops of ribbon. **Chemise** of fine cotton, tucked and embroidered. **Petticoat** of brown, red, and yellow checked silk, quilted, with a brown checked linen top and two ruffles of the silk.

67-68-69
AUSTRIAN, towards the end of the 1860's

67—Color Plate
Purple silk dress. The dress is of heaviest grosgrain silk, trimmed on the waist, sleeve, and bottom of the skirt with bands of black satin ribbon, and embroidered with feathers and bowknots of chenille. The ornament adds richness to the dress. The bodice is simple, tightly cut with a fairly sloping shoulder; the sleeves open at the wrist over an undersleeve and are trimmed at the edge with a rich chenille fringe. A white embroidered collar is worn at the neck.

68—Accessories
Chemise of fine muslin trimmed with tucks, frills. **Corset** of lilac silk, steel-hooked front closing, back lacing. **Drawers** of fine cotton, gathered at the knee into bands, with embroidered ruffles. **Petticoat** of mohair, with box-pleated frill, gathered into a pointed yoke that buttons in the back. **Shoes,** bronze kid, buttoned, with bow at the instep.

69—Pattern Plate

70-71
FRENCH, decade of the 1870's

70—Color Plate

Dress of pink silk. The silk is a heavy faille taffeta of the strongest shade of pink. It is trimmed with bound bias bands of itself, ruffles, and deep, heavy, knotted pink silk fringe. It is more like upholstery than dressmaking, but with all its ugliness has style and magnificence.

71—Accessories

Bustle of heavy white twill, buttoned down the front; stiffened and extended in back with whalebone let into casings. **Corset** of white silk and cotton material, boned with steel-hooked front closing and back lacing. **Chemise** of fine white linen, with real Valenciennes-lace trimming, machine-sewn. **Drawers,** the same. **Petticoat,** the same. **Hair arrangement,** elaborate with curls, puffs, and long tresses, twined with vines of leaves and flowers. **Shoes,** silk with rosette decoration.

72-73
AMERICAN, decade of the 1870's

72—Color Plate

Dress of green taffeta. The silk is a crisp fine taffeta; the color is a vivid apple-green with brilliant lights and deep shades. The dress has an overskirt effect, laid in folds and caught at the sides with straps of the silk ornamented with black velvet buttons. Smaller black velvet buttons are used for the front bodice closing, and a velvet bow is worn at the throat. The collar holds a ruching of net and lace.

73—Accessories

Hair arrangement, known as "the waterfall" because of the structure at the back of the head, which really resembles one. Lots of false hair was used for these. **Shoes** of black kid, with ribbon bows and steel buckles. **Bustle** of crinoline on a cotton foundation. **Petticoat** of cotton, trimmed with lace and shirred puffs. **Corset** of figured cotton material. **Corset waist** of fine nainsook, trimmed with lace and puffings.

74-75
AMERICAN, decade of the 1870's

74—Color Plate

Dress of gray taffeta. The silk is a crisp, heavy, pearl-gray taffeta, trimmed with fringed pleatings and puffings of the same quality of silk in lilac color. The use of two colors of the same silk is typical of many dresses of this period.

75—Accessories

Hair arrangement, elaborate with puffs, braids, and curls, much of it false. **Bustle** of horsehair built on a wire frame. **Chemise** of fine muslin, trimmed with tucks and lace. **Drawers** of muslin, trimmed with tucks and lace. **Corset** of blue silk, embroidered at the top, with ribbon binding. **Shoes** of gray kid, with gray silk trimming, and embroidered. **Petticoat** of gray silk, with embroidered bands and pleated ruffles.

76-77-78-79
AMERICAN, about 1880

76—Color Plate

Red silk dress. The silk is a heavy plain silk. The bodice is long and tight, with many seams, and fits close to the body. From the hips down the dress is over-trimmed with puffs, ruffles, overskirts, back draperies, and fringe. It spreads out into a long train and requires a lot of material for the making. The form of the dress was commonly known as the "lobster pot," and is interesting as coming between the periods of the two types of exaggerated bustles.

77—Accessories

Chemise of muslin, tucked, stitched, and trimmed with lace. **Petticoat** of heavy muslin. The back section, or train, is detachable and buttons onto the petticoat itself. The ruffles and insertion are of machine embroidery. **Drawers** of cotton, with lace and embroidery bands. **Corset** of fancy-weave cotton, boned and beautifully hand-embroidered. It has a steel-hooked front closing and a back lacing.

78—Accessories

Underpetticoat of flannel, embroidered with silk thread. **Hair arrangement** is soft and becoming, parted and worn in puffs. **Bustle,** long and flat, made of cotton and metal. **Shoes** of black kid, cut out at the instep, and laced with ribbon and trimmed with bows.

79—Pattern Plate

80-81-82-83
AMERICAN, decade of the 1880's

80—Color Plate

Gray silk dress. The dress is made of part moire, part faille. The bodice is tightly cut, with many seams; it buttons down the center front and is worn over the skirt. The back has long tabs, and the cut is known as the postilion. The skirt is built out very long at the back over a bustle, tremendously extended, and weighted with a pleated overskirt and all sorts of pleatings and ruffles. It is ugly, but splendid.

81—Accessories

Hair arrangement is parted and drawn to a soft roll at the back. **Bonnet** of gray felt, with feather and ribbon trimming. **Dolman** of black wool with fur trimming. Cut to fit the bustle. **Shoes** are black kid, low-cut and buttoned. **Bustle** of cotton, buttoned at the front and stiffened with whalebone.

82—Accessories

Corset of heavy white figured stuff, boned, and embroidered. Steel-hooked front closing, back lacing. **Chemise** of nainsook, trimmed with lace, puffing, and beading. **Drawers** of nainsook and lace, trimmed with ribbons at the knee. **Petticoat** of muslin, a deep curved yoke that buttons at the back, trimmed with tucks and embroidery. There is a detachable piece that buttons on at the back edge, to go under the train of the dress and protect it from dust. Drawstrings hold the skirt tight at the back.

83—Partial Pattern Plate

2 · ENGLISH · ABOUT 1700–1710

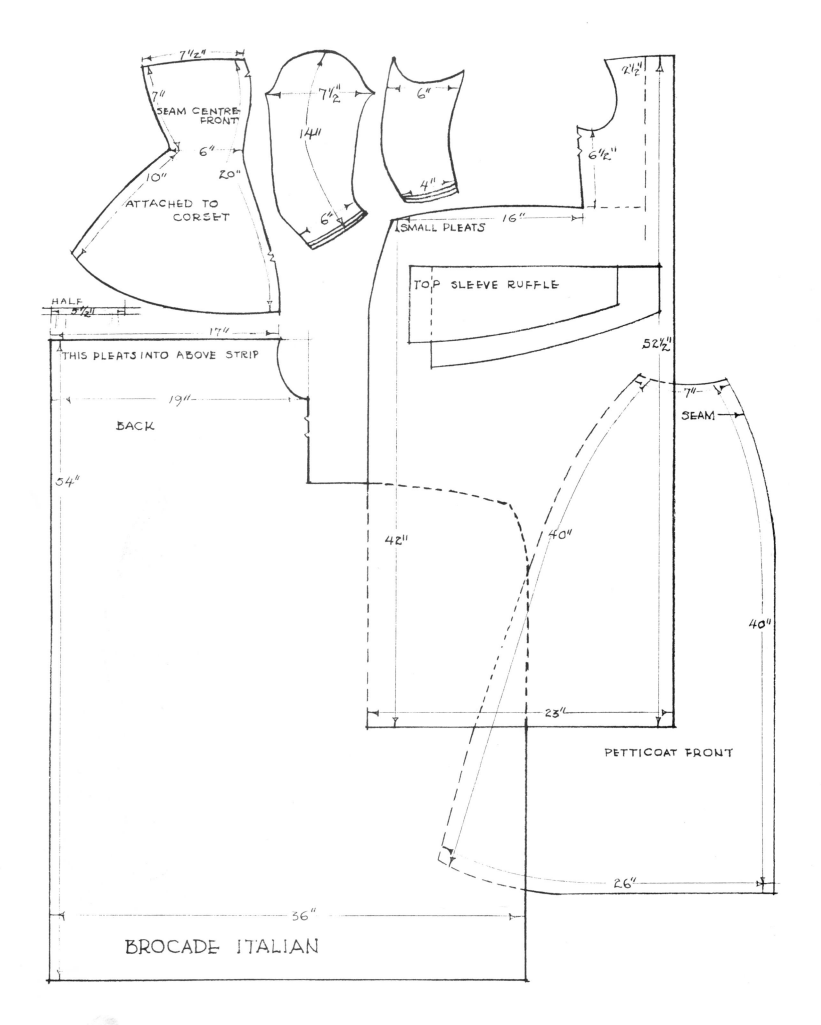

7½"

7"

SEAM CENTRE FRONT

6"

10"

20"

ATTACHED TO CORSET

7½"

14"

6"

6"

4"

2½"

6½"

SMALL PLEATS

16"

TOP SLEEVE RUFFLE

HALF
5½"

17"

THIS PLEATS INTO ABOVE STRIP

19"

BACK

54"

52½"

7"

SEAM

42"

40"

40"

23"

PETTICOAT FRONT

26"

36"

BROCADE ITALIAN

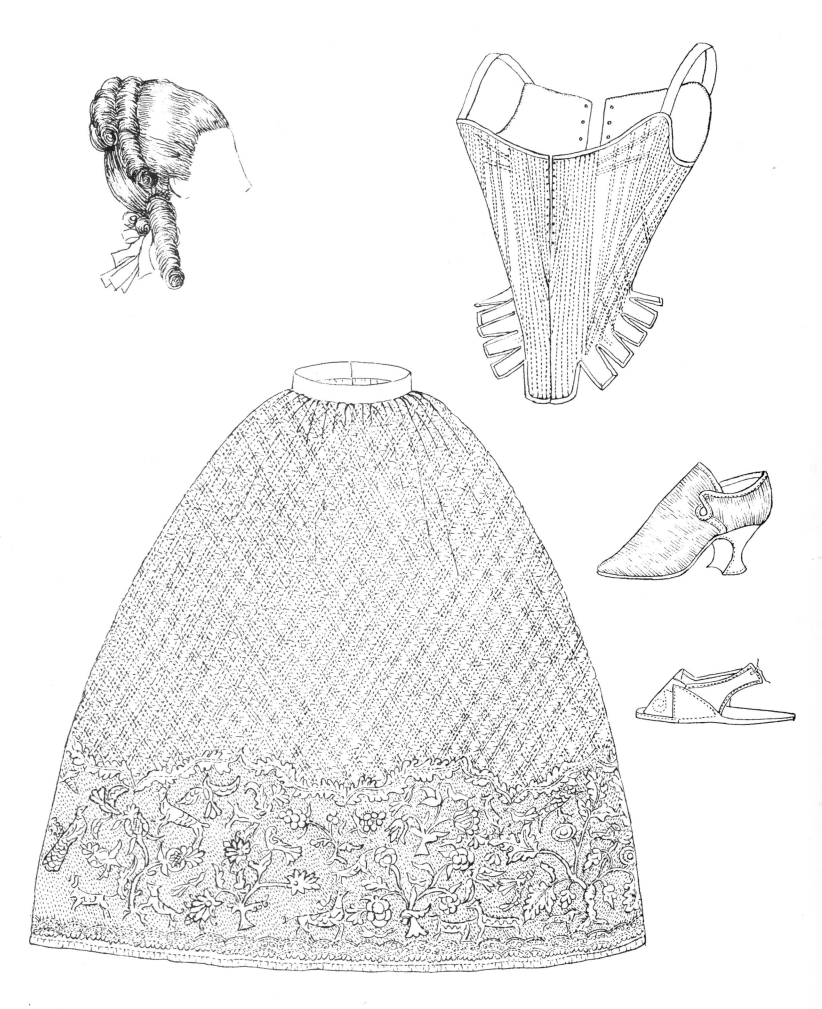

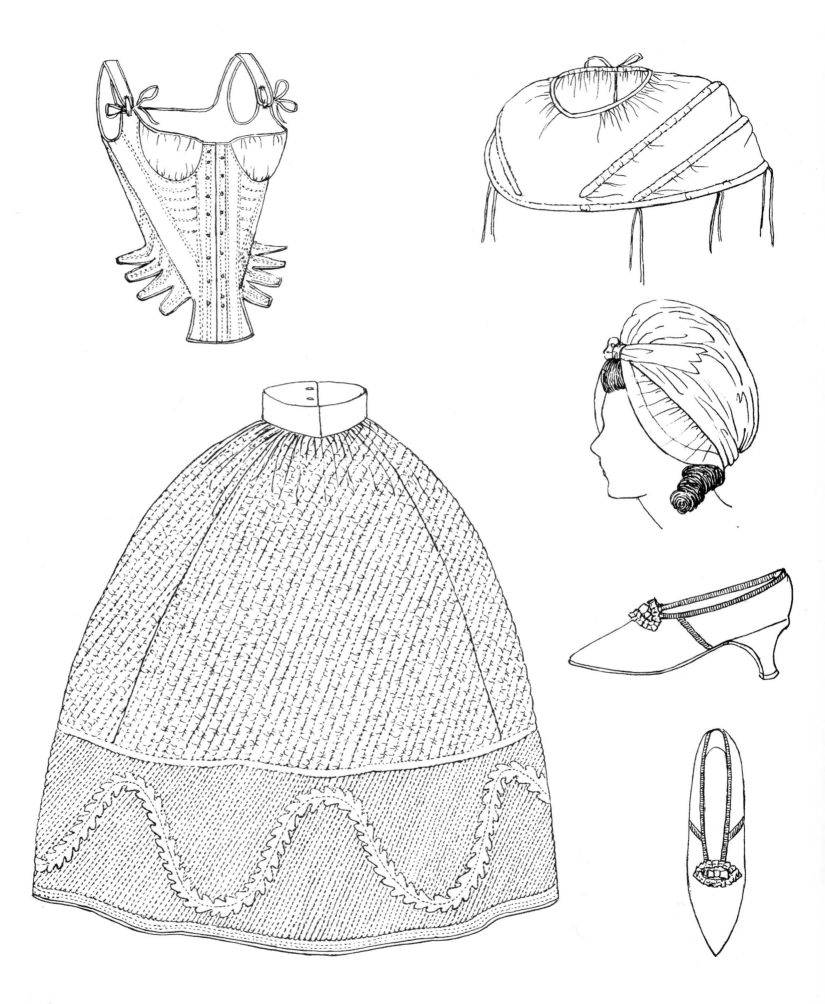

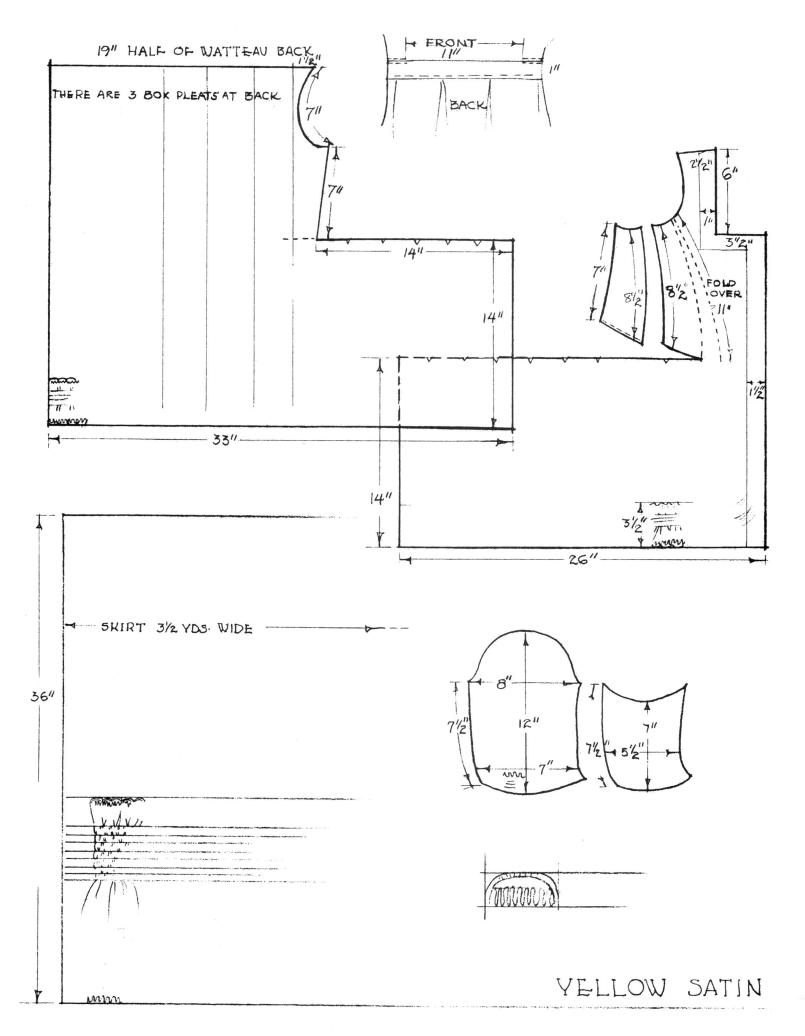

19" HALF OF WATTEAU BACK

1'½"

THERE ARE 3 BOX PLEATS AT BACK

FRONT
11"

BACK

1"

7"

7"

2'½"

6"

1"

3'½"

14"

FOLD OVER

7"

8'½"

8'½"

11"

14"

1'½"

33"

14"

3'½"

26"

SKIRT 3½ YDS. WIDE

36"

8"

7'½"

12"

7"

7'½"

5'½"

7"

YELLOW SATIN

14 · ENGLISH · LAST HALF OF THE 18TH CENTURY

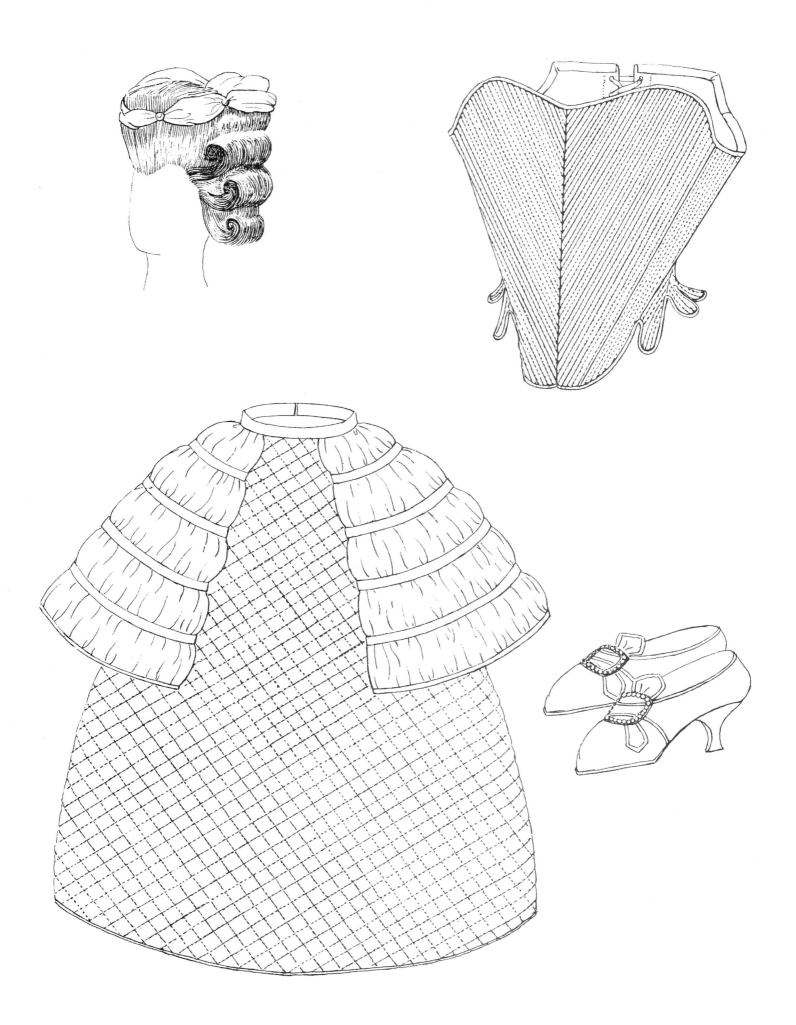

18 · ENGLISH · LAST QUARTER OF THE 18TH CENTURY

20 · FRENCH · VERY END OF THE 18TH CENTURY

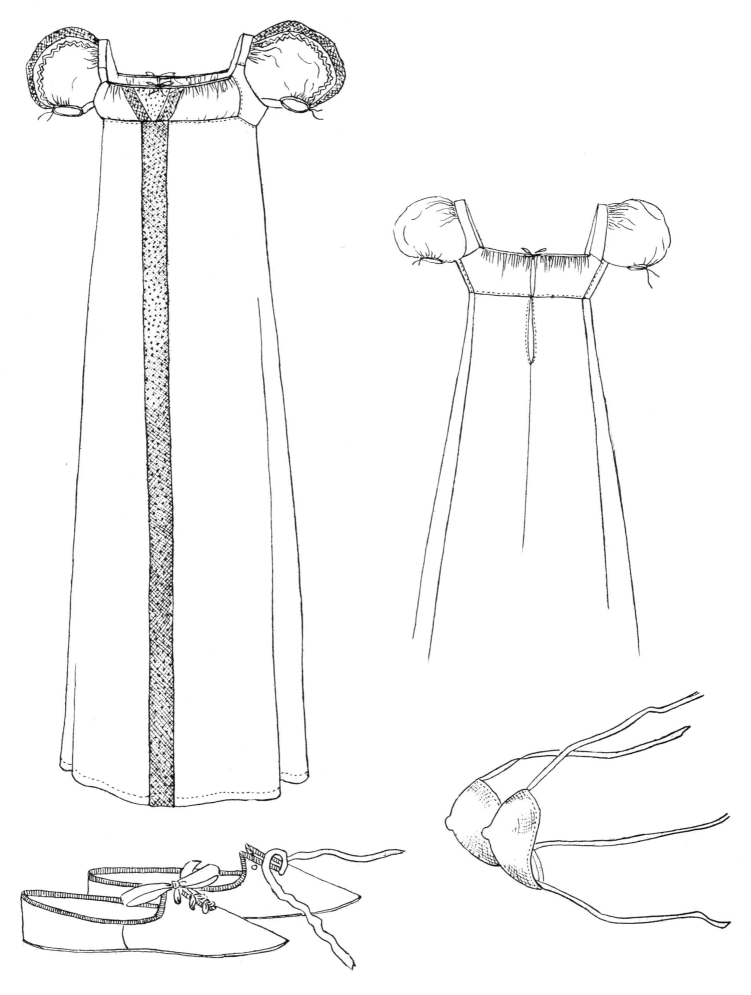

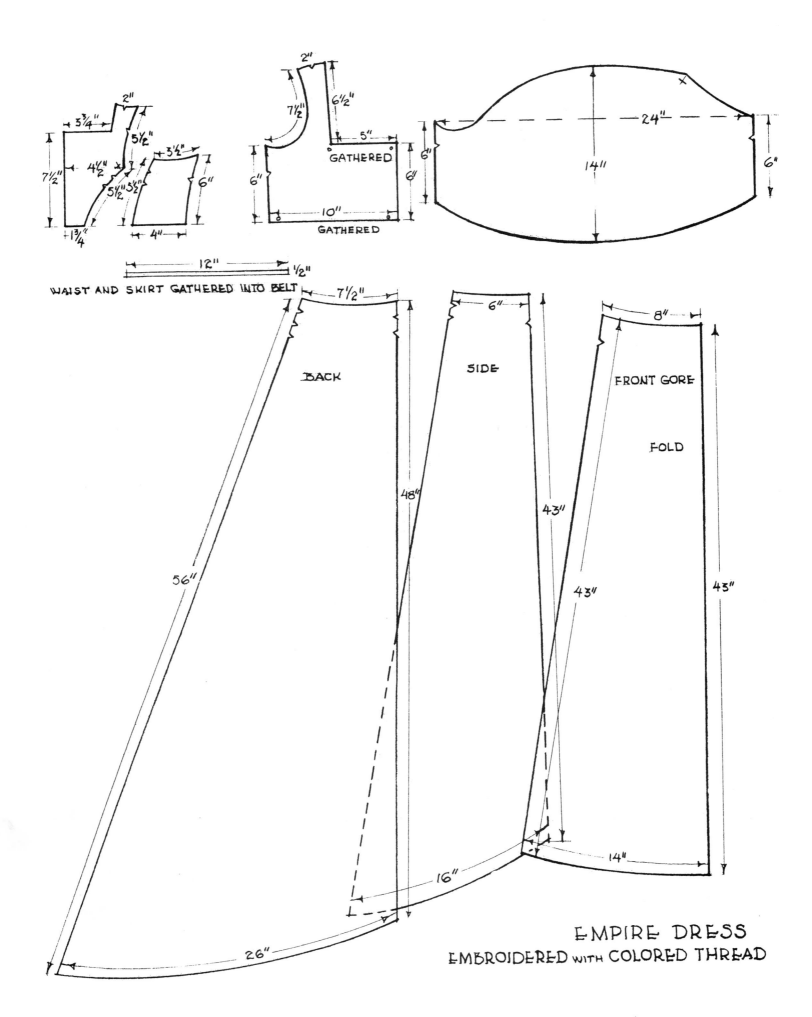

WAIST AND SKIRT GATHERED INTO BELT

GATHERED

GATHERED

BACK

SIDE

FRONT GORE

FOLD

EMPIRE DRESS
EMBROIDERED WITH COLORED THREAD

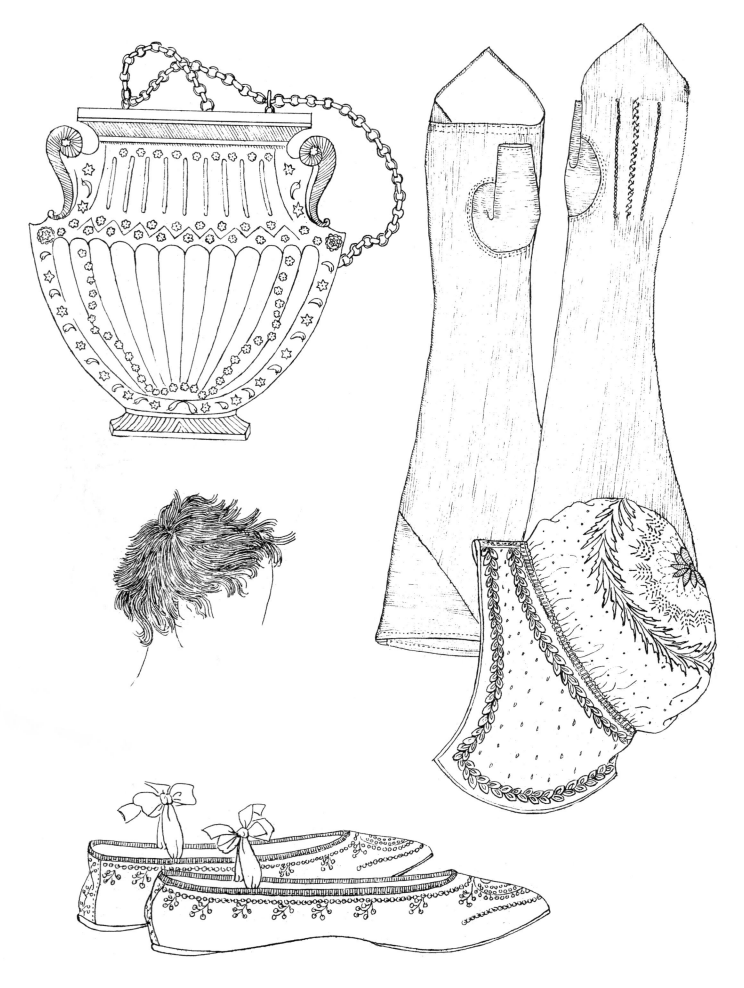

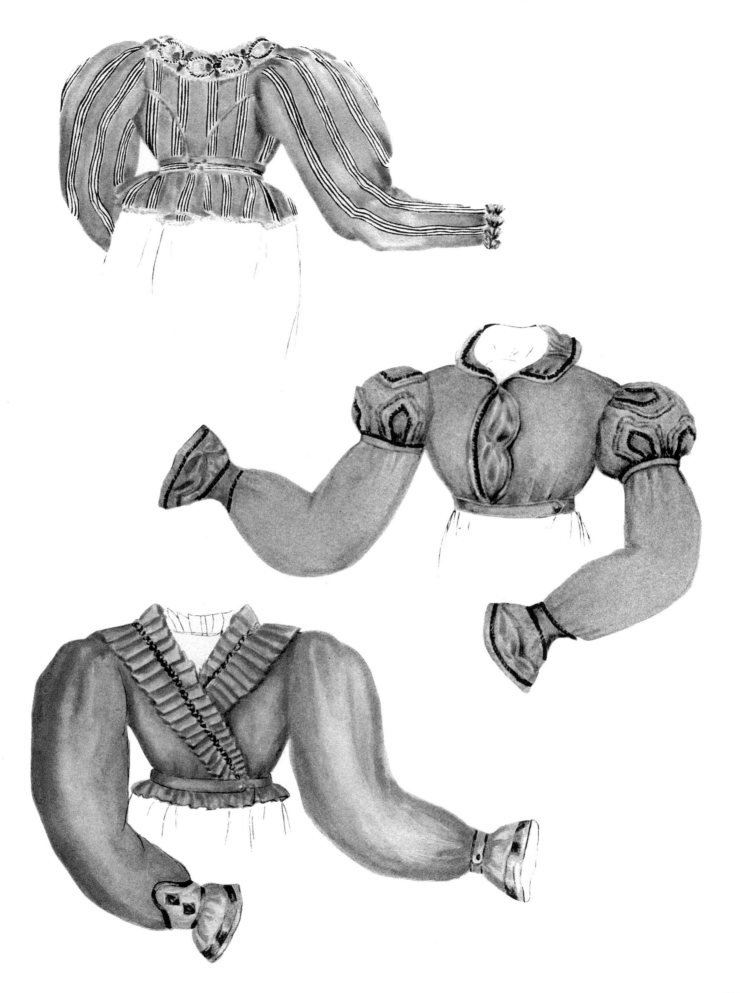

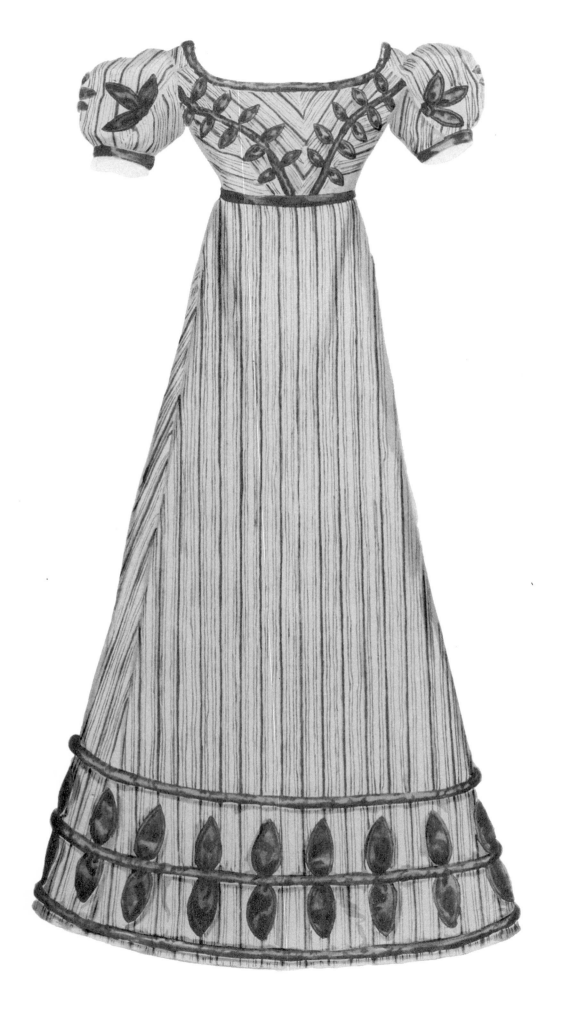

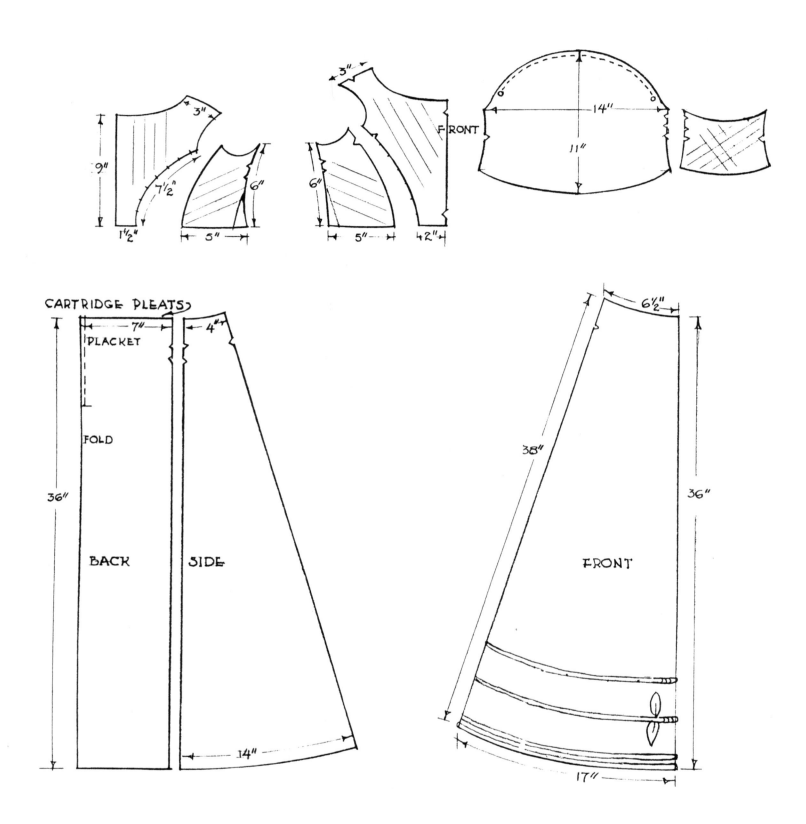

BLUE AND WHITE STRIPED SILK

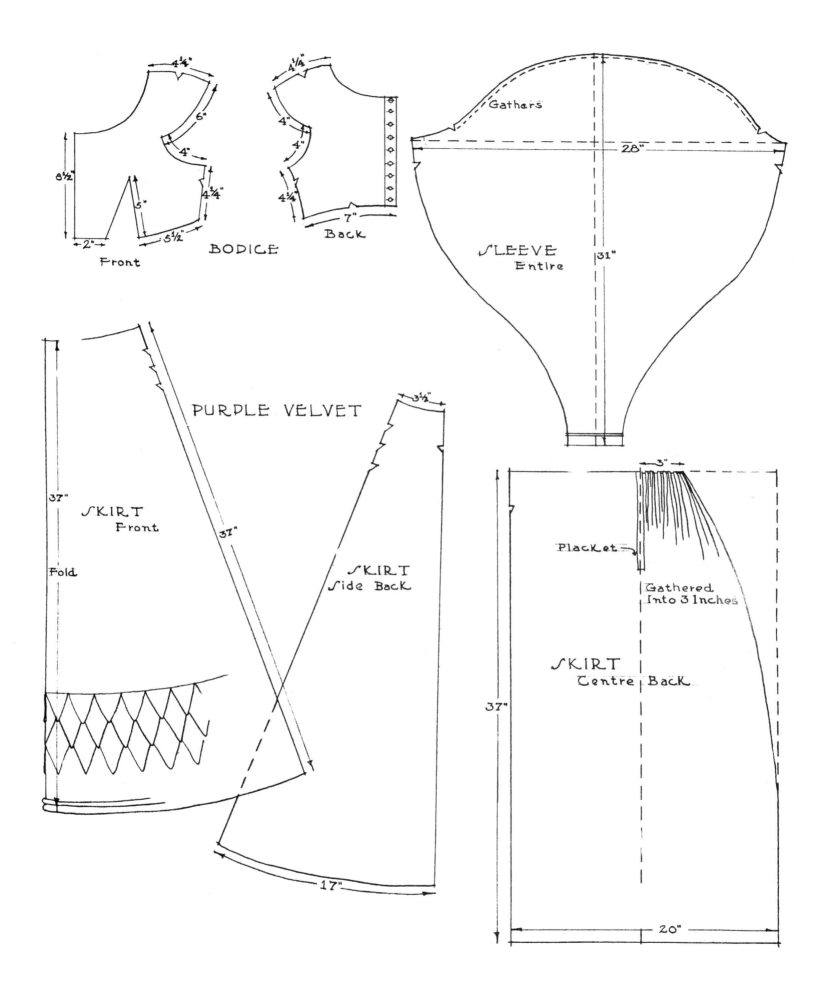

4¼"

6"

4"

4"

8½"

5"

2"

5½"

4¼"

Front

BODICE

4¼"
4"
4"

4¼"

7"

Back

Gathers

28"

SLEEVE
Entire

31"

PURPLE VELVET

3½"

37"

SKIRT
Front

37"

Fold

SKIRT
Side Back

17"

3"

Placket

Gathered
Into 3 Inches

SKIRT
Centre Back

37"

20"

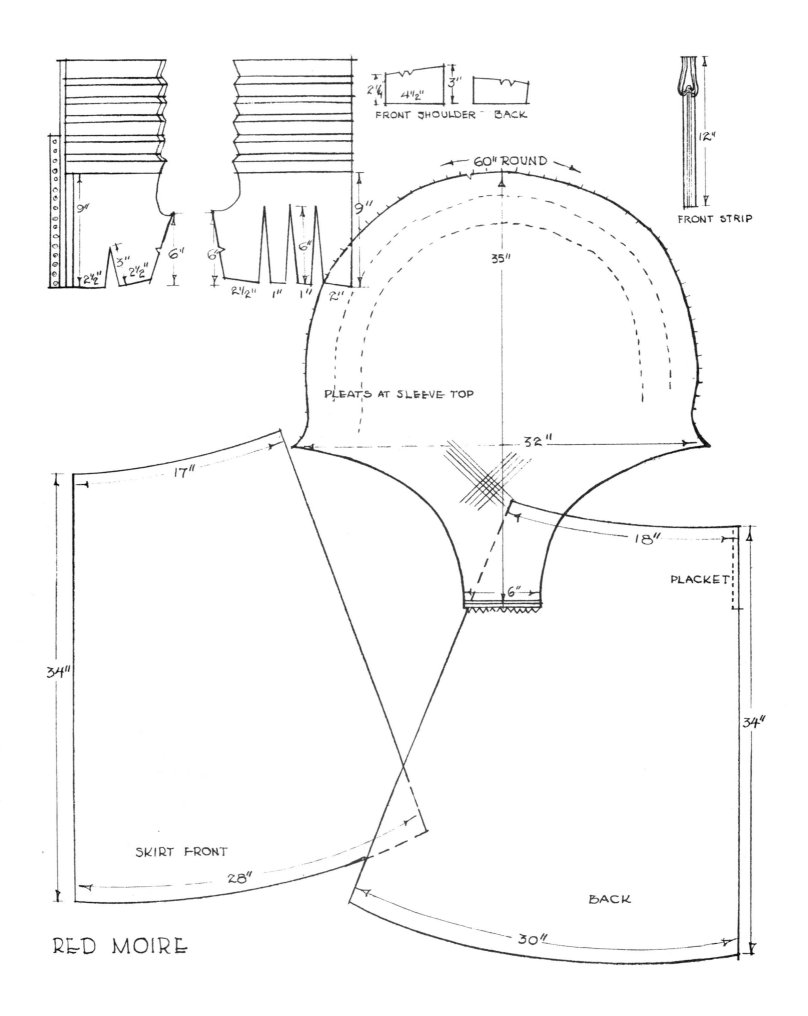

FRONT SHOULDER · BACK

60" ROUND

FRONT STRIP

12"

PLEATS AT SLEEVE TOP

35"

32"

17"

18"

PLACKET

34"

34"

SKIRT FRONT

28"

BACK

6"

30"

RED MOIRE

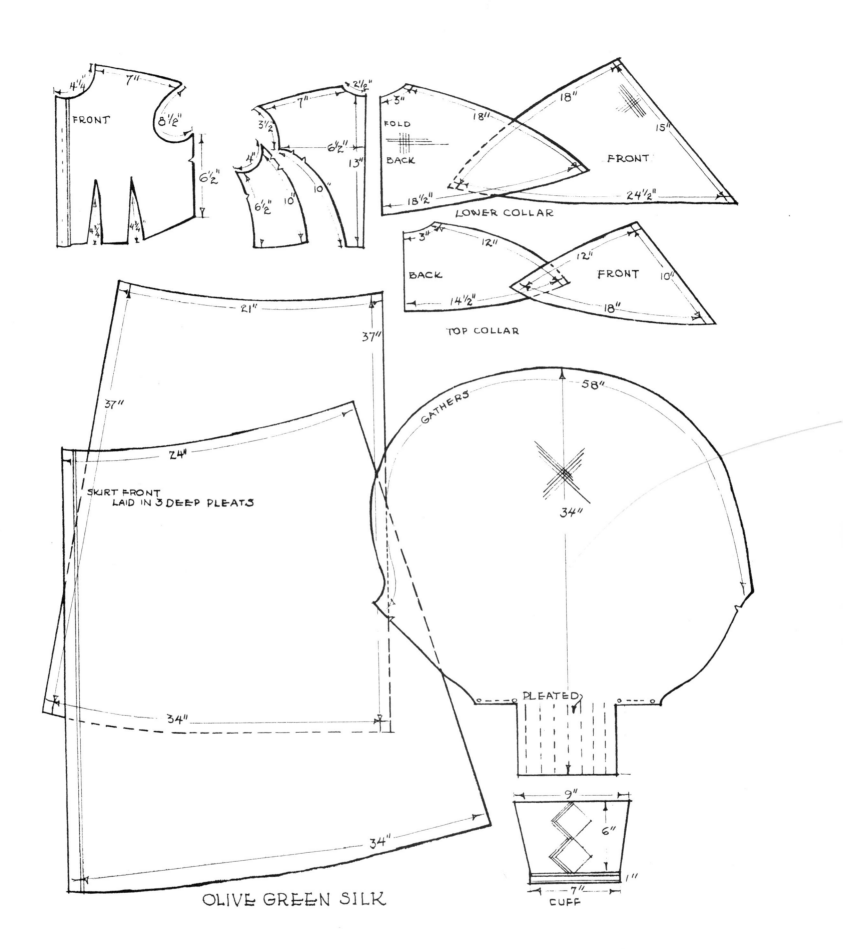

FRONT

FOLD

BACK

LOWER COLLAR

FRONT

BACK

FRONT

TOP COLLAR

SKIRT FRONT
LAID IN 3 DEEP PLEATS

GATHERS

PLEATED

CUFF

OLIVE GREEN SILK

44 · AMERICAN · ABOUT 1845

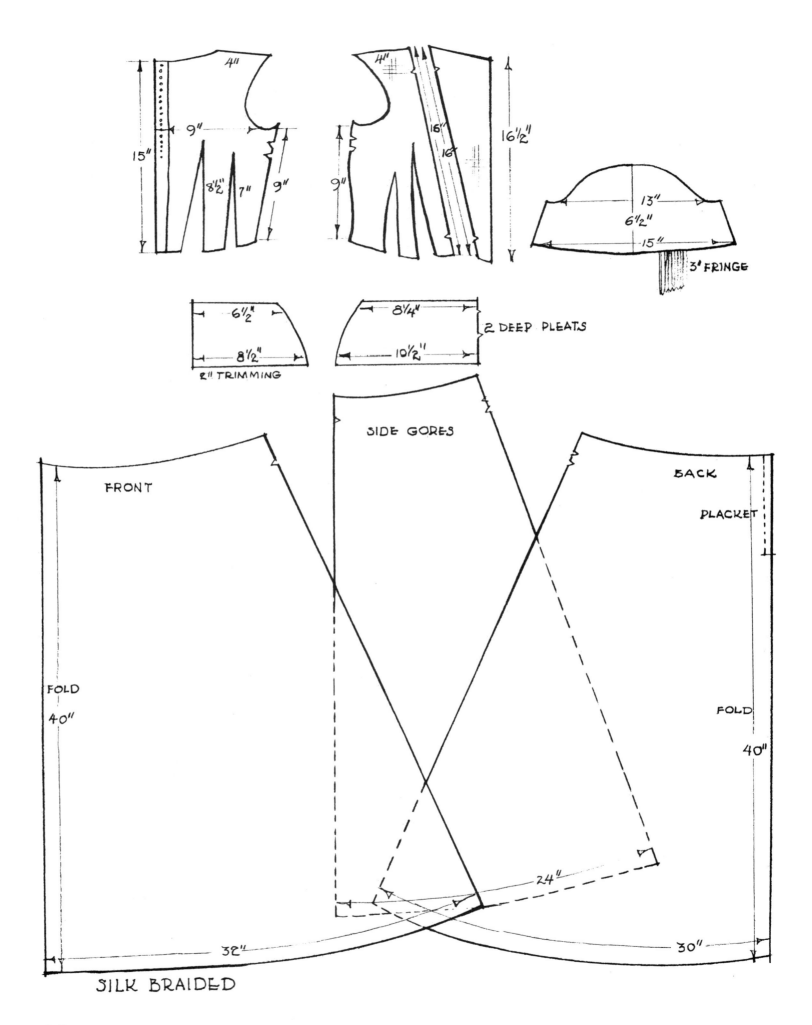

4"

9"

15"

8½" 7" 9"

4"

16"

16

16½"

9"

13"

6½"

15"

3' FRINGE

6½"

8½"

8" TRIMMING

8¼"

10½"

2 DEEP PLEATS

SIDE GORES

FRONT

BACK

PLACKET

FOLD
40"

FOLD
40"

24"

32"

30"

SILK BRAIDED

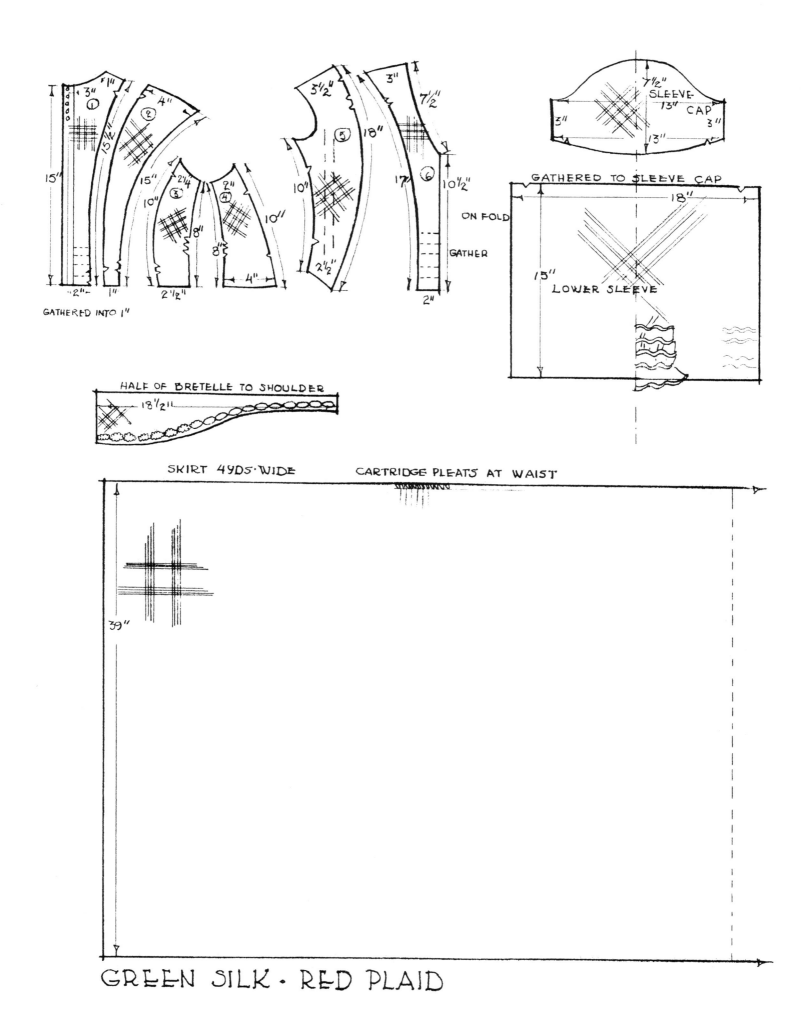

GATHERED INTO 1"

HALF OF BRETELLE TO SHOULDER

18½"

SLEEVE CAP

7½"
13"
3"
3"
13"

GATHERED TO SLEEVE CAP

18"

15"

LOWER SLEEVE

ON FOLD

GATHER

SKIRT 4 YDS. WIDE   CARTRIDGE PLEATS AT WAIST

39"

GREEN SILK · RED PLAID

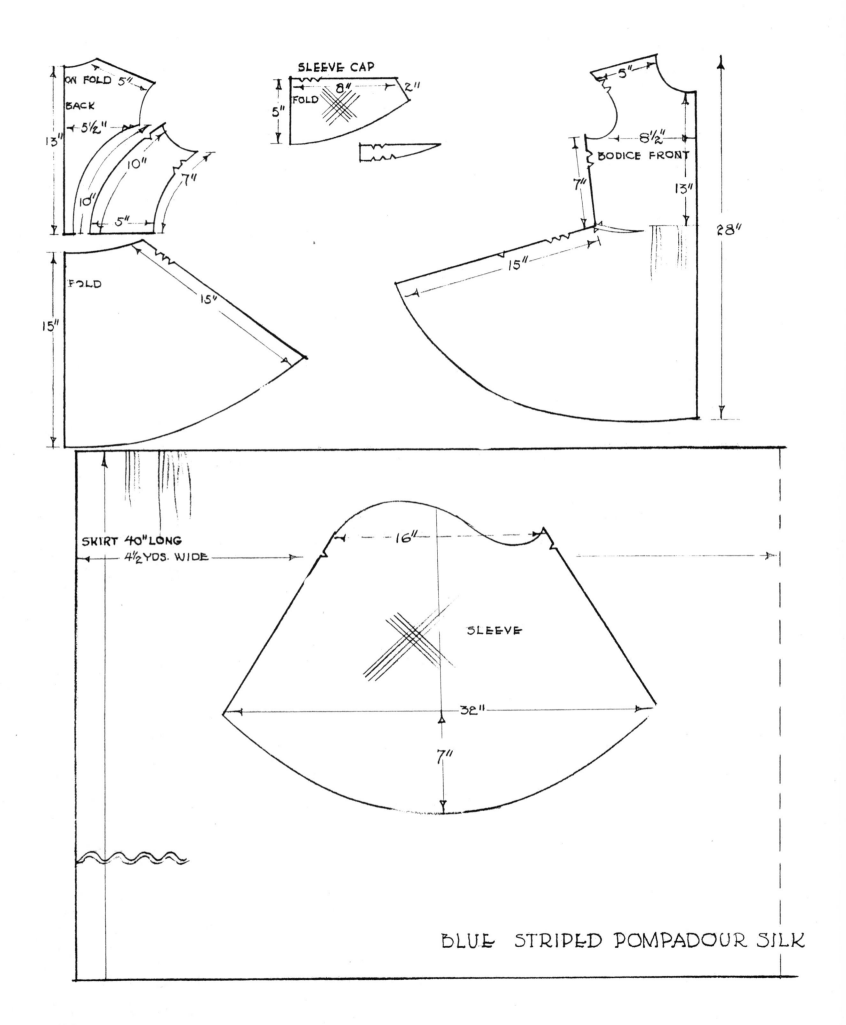

ON FOLD 5"

BACK

13"

5½"

10"

10"

5"

7"

SLEEVE CAP

8"

2"

5"

FOLD

5"

FOLD

15"

15"

5"

8½"

BODICE FRONT

7"

13"

28"

15"

SKIRT 40" LONG
4½ YDS. WIDE

16"

SLEEVE

32"

7"

BLUE STRIPED POMPADOUR SILK

Plate 1

Plate 3

Plate 7

Plate 9

Plate 11

Plate 14

Plate 16

Plate 18

Plate 20

Plate 22

Plate 24

Plate 27

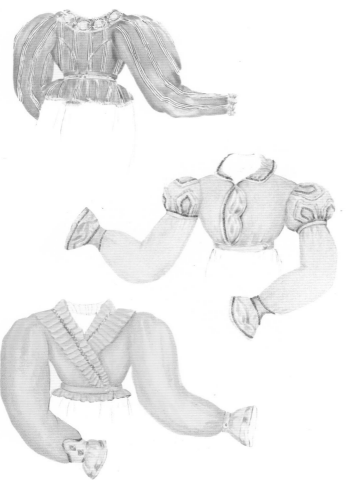

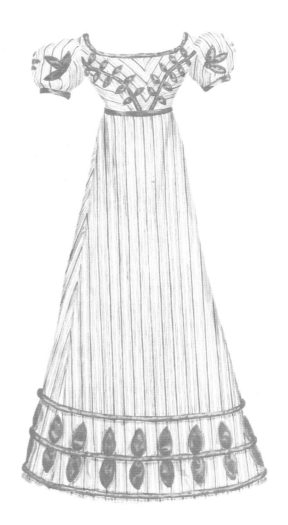

Plate 29

Plate 30

Plate 33

Plate 36

Plate 39

Plate 41

Plate 44

Plate 47

Plate 50

Plate 53

Plate 55

Plate 59

Plate 62

Plate 64

Plate 67

Plate 70

Plate 72

Plate 74

Plate 76

Plate 80

56 · FRENCH · ABOUT 1858

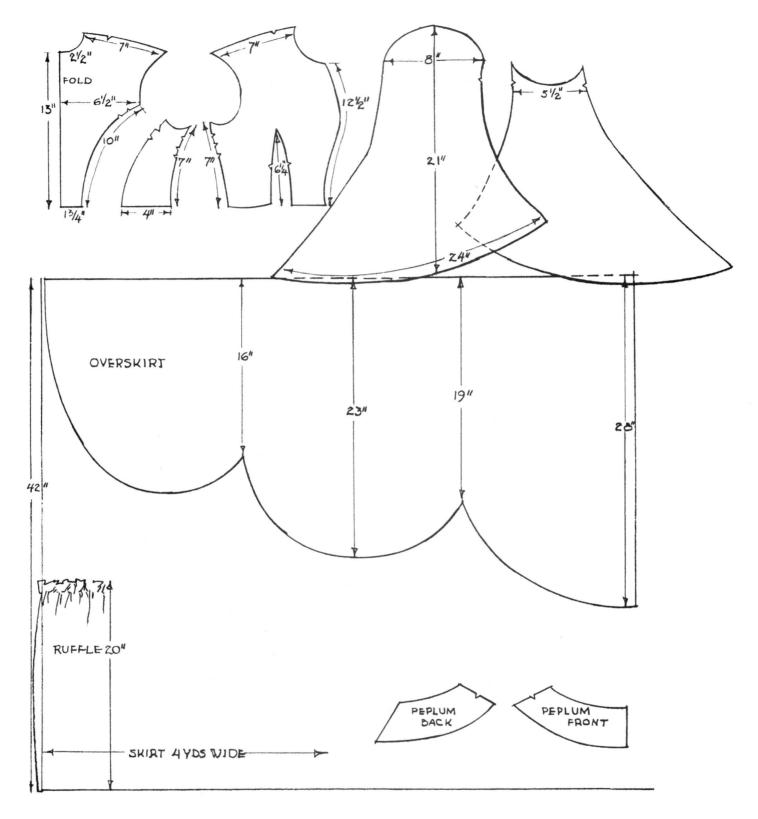

2½"

FOLD

7"

7"

8"

5½"

13"

6½"

12½"

21"

10"

7"   7"

6¼"

1¾"

4"

24"

OVERSKIRT

16"

23"

19"

28"

42"

RUFFLE 20"

PEPLUM
BACK

PEPLUM
FRONT

SKIRT 4 YDS WIDE

YELLOW SILK
BROWN VELVET FLOWERS

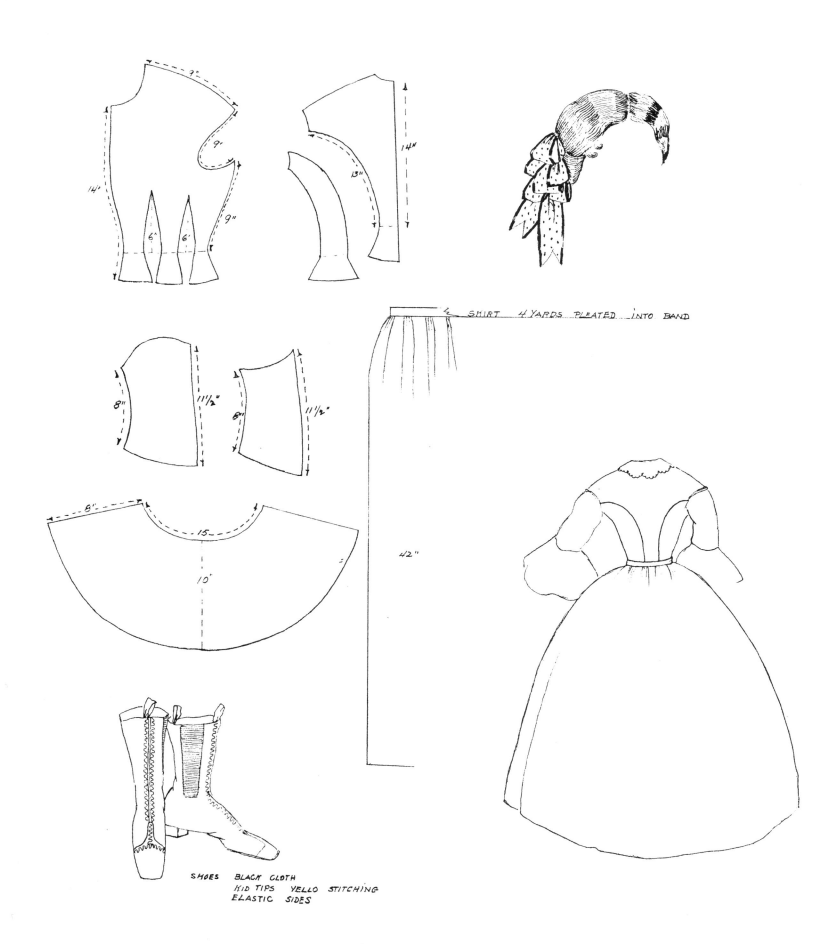

SHIRT 4 YARDS PLEATED INTO BAND

SHOES BLACK CLOTH
KID TIPS YELLO STITCHING
ELASTIC SIDES

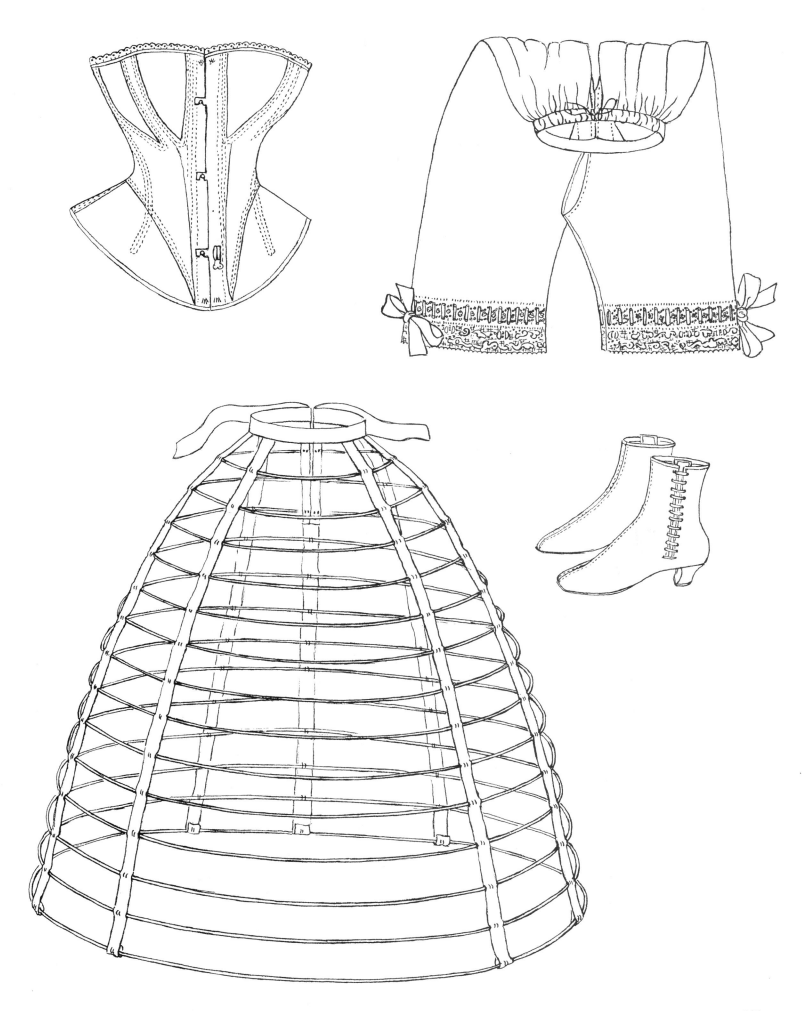

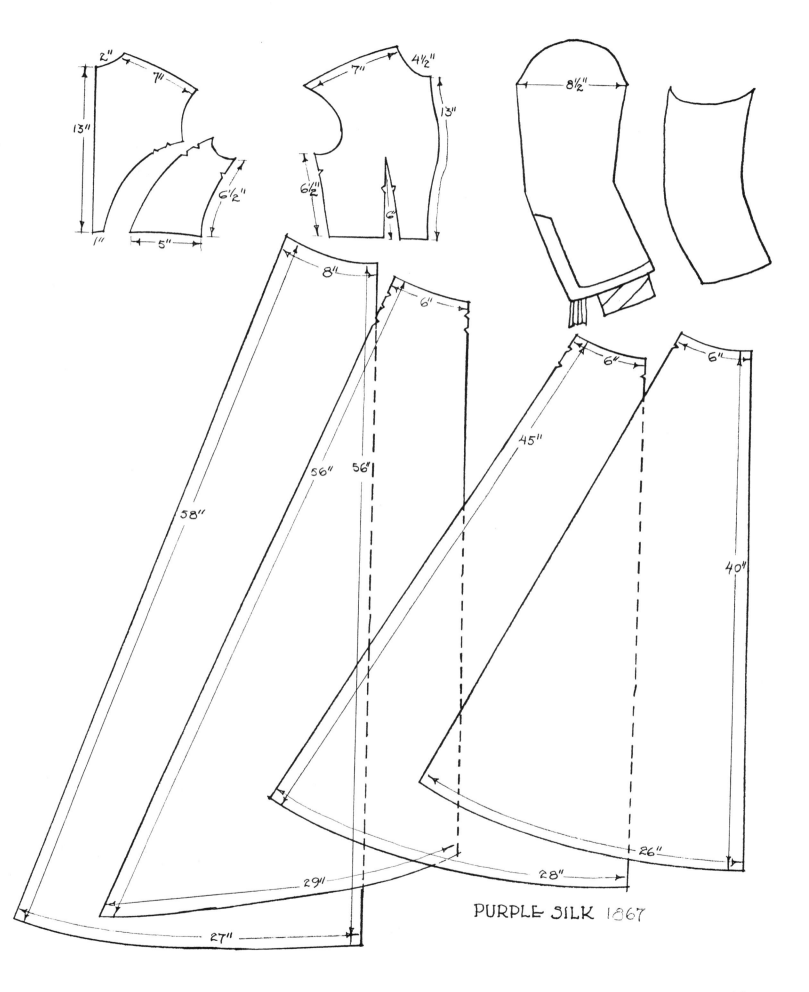

PURPLE SILK 1867

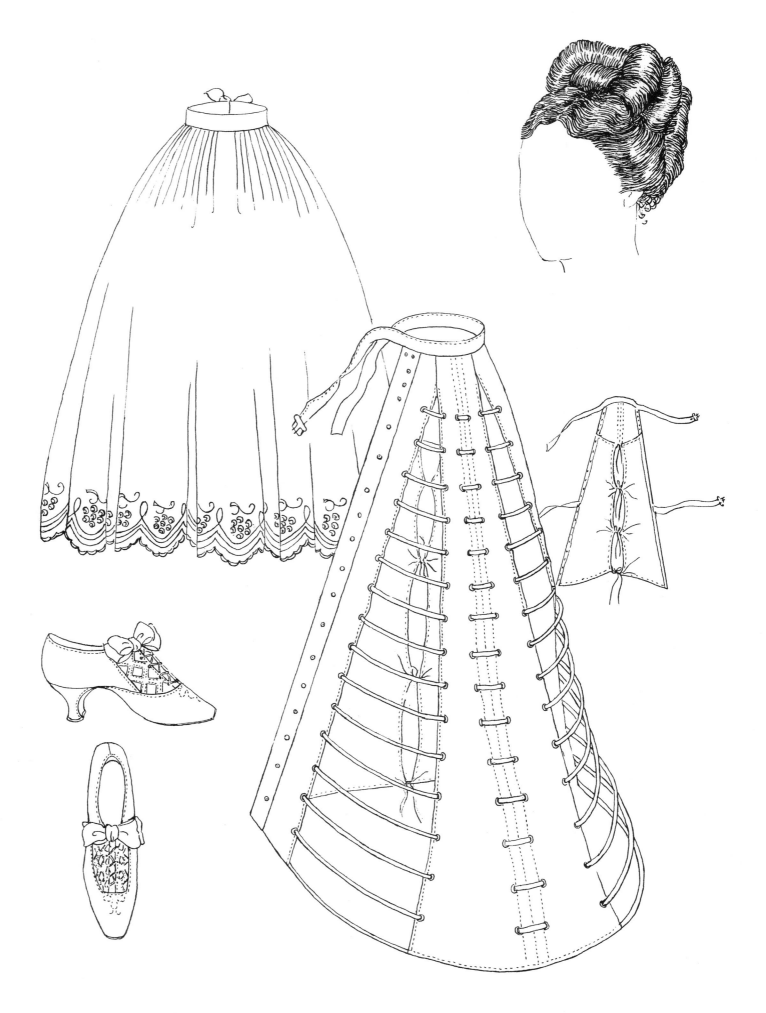

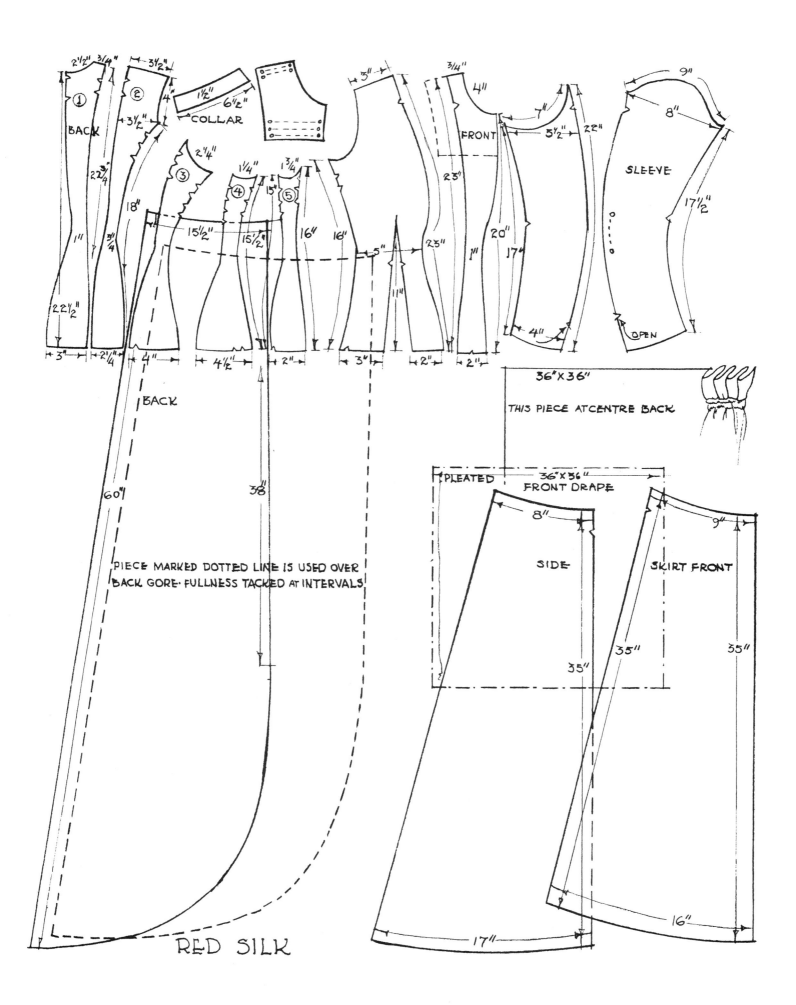

2½" ¾" 3½"
① ②
BACK
3½"
4"
COLLAR 1½"
6½"
2¼"
③
22¾"
④ 1¼" 3¼"
⑤
15" 15"
1"
18"
15½"
15½" 16" 16"
22½" 5"
11"

3" 2¼" 4" 4½" 2" 3" 2" 2"

BACK

60"

38"

PIECE MARKED DOTTED LINE IS USED OVER
BACK GORE. FULLNESS TACKED AT INTERVALS

RED SILK

3"
FRONT
¾" 4"
7"
5½" 22"
23"
20"
1" 17"
4"

SLEEVE
9"
8"
17½"
OPEN

36"X36"
THIS PIECE AT CENTRE BACK

PLEATED 36"X36"
FRONT DRAPE
8" 9"
SIDE SKIRT FRONT
35" 35" 35"
17" 16"

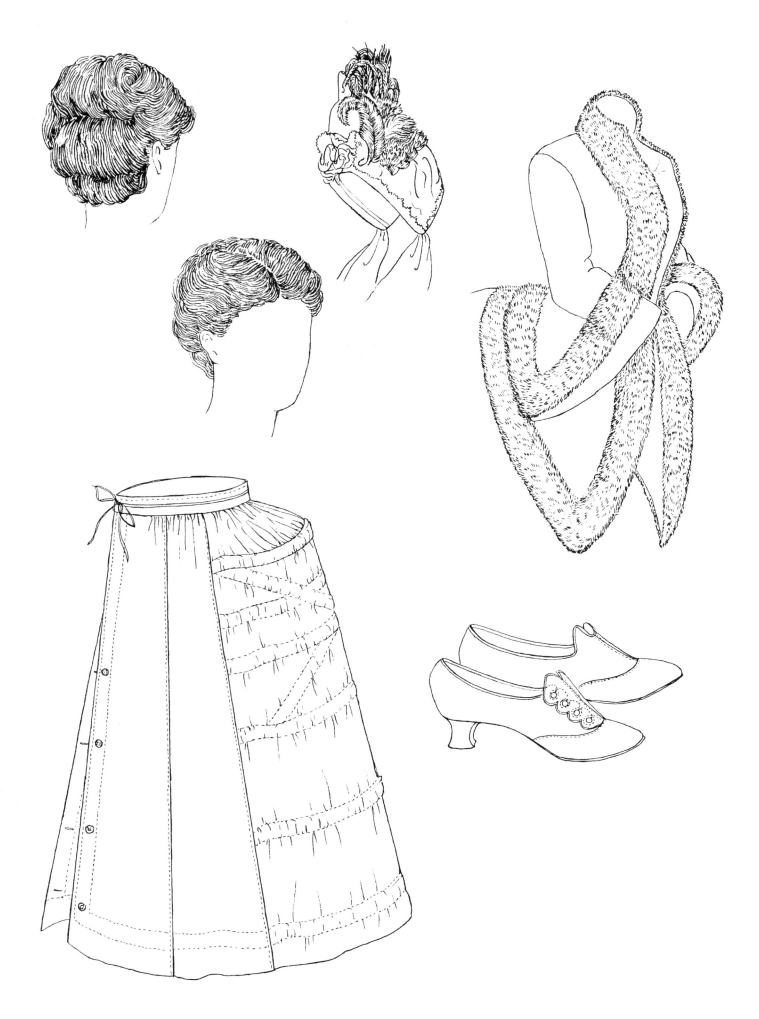

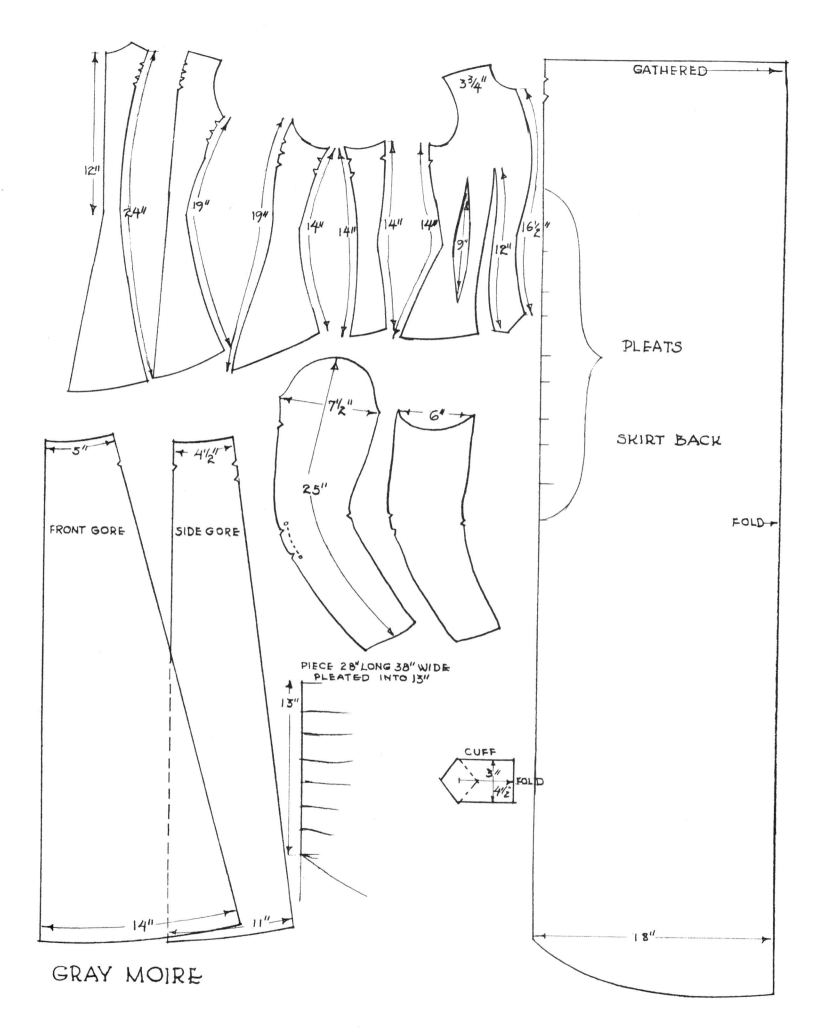

GATHERED

12"

24" 19" 19" 14" 14" 14" 14" 3¾" 9" 12" 16½"

PLEATS

7½" 6"

SKIRT BACK

25"

5" 4½"

FRONT GORE SIDE GORE

FOLD

PIECE 28" LONG 38" WIDE
PLEATED INTO 13"

13"

CUFF

3"
FOLD
4½"

14" 11"

18"

GRAY MOIRE